The Art

OF War

Simplified

简单

VINCENT GAGLIANO

ASPIRE
PUBLISHING HUB LLC.

The Art of War Simplified
Copyright © 2022 by Vincent Gagliano

ISBN
978-1-958692-34-9 (Paperback)
978-1-958692-35-6 (eBook)

Table of Contents

Preface v

Acknowledgments ix

Chapter 1   Planning 1

Chapter 2   Fighting 7

Chapter 3   Strategically Attacking........................... 12

Chapter 4   Tactics 19

Chapter 5   Energy 24

Chapter 6   Weak Points and Strong.......................... 31

Chapter 7   Maneuvering... 39

Chapter 8   Varying Tactics 45

Chapter 9   The Marching Army.............................. 48

Chapter 10   Battleground.. 53

Chapter 11   The Nine Types of Turf 58

Chapter 12   Attack with Fire 69

Chapter 13   Spying 73

Conclusion.. 77

About the Author.. 79

Bibliography.. 80

Notes 84

Preface

In 2005, I was a high school student when I first came upon Sun Tzu's book, *The Art of War*. I had purchased a copy and looked forward to reading it in my spare time that day. A piece of literary history dating back 2,500 years was at my fingertips. What nuggets of truth would the book have in store for an avid chess student, the world's oldest, most famous, and least chance-dependent military game?

I cracked open the book, read it from cover to cover, and... was disappointed.

Looking back, I probably should have known that the lessons in the book weren't always obvious, at least at first. Josh Waitzkin, the subject of the movie *Searching for Bobby Fischer* and the author of *The Art of Learning*, would later write that this was typical of Far Eastern proverbs, where the lessons would make you sit and digest their true meanings. Even in the movie *The Karate Kid* (the 1984 version, not the remake), Mr. Miyagi's methods of teaching Daniel martial arts seemed to make no sense whatsoever. What did waxing cars have to do with karate that, say, breaking boards didn't?

But at the time, this was of no help to me whatsoever, especially not to a teenager who was more gifted at math than a Chinese scholar. So, I gave up, gave the book to the school, and moved on with my life.

Five years later, I was home from college at the University of Florida for the summer. I had taken an interest in learning all I could about leadership. I was well aware that I did not have the savviest business instincts and was looking for something I could read that would help me. While skimming through the titles, I came across *The Art of War for Managers,* written by Gerald A. Michaelson and his son, Steve. As I flipped through the pages, both men took the passages I had read back in high school and explained them in ways I could understand. I was hooked and bought a copy of the original through Amazon.

Then one day, while I was sitting on my bed reading, inspiration struck.

Many books on *The Art of War* that cater to a broader audience are academic translations like what I read the first time, and many of the books that explain these concepts clearly target niche markets. What was the chance I would have read *The Art of War for Managers* if I wasn't interested in management or leadership?

Why not craft a book that was both for a broad audience *and* explained Sun Tzu's concepts clearly? Hence, *The Art of War Simplified* was born.

Unlike many other books based on *The Art of War*, *The Art of War Simplified* is in no way intended to be a scholarly, word-for-word translation of the original Chinese text. It also takes the opposite approach to a scholarly translation with commentary, which provides the translation in addition to more wording to help explain the concepts.

My intent is to stick to the spirit and background of the original book while boiling down the statements in the original to more basic concepts. Also, because I would have greatly appreciated it in the original, I will give you a plan to help study the book and put it to good use because, as I will say in the text, "Just because you *know* how to win doesn't mean you *will* win."

But what makes *The Art of War* an important classic? Why should any edition of this book, whether it is an original translation or an adaptation, stand out in the pile of business or military books offered today?

You can easily envision battle as a military metaphor in virtually any competitive discipline. For example, a top Fortune 500 company is run like a powerful army. The CEO is like the head general, dictating the company's direction. They have considerable resources at their disposal, whether they are tied to their people (soldiers), their advantages in material (supplies), or some other dynamic advantage (initiative, cycle time, and the like). The company routinely fights other companies, or armies, in its industry, but the battleground is its customer's hearts, minds, and ultimately, wallets. Mistakes in strategy or tactics will ultimately result in a loss of sales or worse. Even if the battles now are different than they were back when Sun Tzu wrote the original, the original ideas are still relevant today.

The original version of *The Art of War* is a slice of ancient history, written down and reproduced for future generations to read. And, as the saying goes, history repeats itself. Why not take advantage of this and learn from the past so you can change your future battle plans better?

The Chinese economy is growing at a rapid rate. At the time of this writing, the Chinese economy has become the second largest economy in the world, and a poll conducted by the BBC predicts that it will surpass the United States as the world's biggest economic superpower by the year 2026. As Americans, it behooves us to learn from and study Chinese culture, and *The Art of War* is one of the most well-known Chinese books.

Finally, the book makes for an interesting change of pace from studying materials that are directly related to your craft. It will challenge you to think in entirely new and different ways about attacking the issues at hand. Have you ever had the experience of thinking long and hard about a problem only to find an epiphany when you think about something entirely different? If nothing else, this book can help facilitate that process since, chances are, military strategy is not related to your original subject.

It is my hope that this book inspires you.

Acknowledgments

Thank you, Ryan Ferguson and Dennis Troyanos, for encouraging me to hone my writing.

Thank you, Attila Vekony, for your advice during this process.

Thank you, Tony C., for empowering me.

Thank you to all my teachers. I know I probably wasn't the easiest student to teach, but I still learned.

Most of all, thank you, Lord, for all you have given me.

Chapter One

A bad plan is better than no plan.

Most people wouldn't even think of baking a cake without a recipe, going on a road trip without a map, or building a house without a blueprint. Similarly, to win in whatever competitive discipline you are in, you need to find a way to obtain information about how you will succeed and what obstacles you will face.

Bad planning is not ideal. But if you're planning, you're already taking steps toward achieving your goals, and you can often correct your plans in the future. However, if you have no plan, you have no chance of success because you cannot gauge how close you are to your goal or whether you even have a goal.

War is an art form of utmost importance to a country.

War makes all the difference between living and dying, between your salvation and slaughter. Hence, there is no excuse not to learn about it.

The art of war has its foundation in five different factors, which you must plan for to win. They are:

1. Integrity

2. Outside forces

3. Battleground

4. Leadership

5. Principle

Leaders with *integrity* make people believe in them. People will follow a leader with integrity even unto death, regardless of trials.

Outside forces are those factors that affect you that are out of your control. In combat, the weather can turn on you and cause difficulties for your army. In business, the economic climate can change at a moment's notice. In sports, it's the big play that suddenly shifts momentum.

The *battleground* is the place where you will fight your battles. In chess, the chessboard is the battleground; in politics, all campaigns aim to gain more votes than the competition; and in business, companies design the best marketing strategies to influence customers to buy their products.

People who exhibit good *leadership* are sincere, kind, brave, wise, and disciplined.

Principles are those rules that help you make decisions about what to do. Often, you learn principles about life when you are growing up. You can also learn principles as you gain experience in your line of work. This book teaches you the principles of battle.

Every general needs to know these five factors. Know them, and you will win. Ignore them, and you will lose.

If you want to know if you will win a battle, ask yourself seven questions:

1. Which ruler has more integrity? If rulers do not have integrity, their soldiers will not be able to trust them because they can't be confident that their leader will do the right thing. It is possible to win a battle or two if you lack the integrity of your opponent. But, over time, the lack of trust that your soldiers have in you will continue to escalate until it manifests itself on the battlefield, leading to both their undoing and yours.

2. Which general is more capable?

3. Which side is better supported by outside forces and the battleground?

4. Which side is more disciplined?

5. Which army has more resources or personnel?

6. Which side has better-trained personnel?

7. Which army does a better job enforcing justice? If leaders are unjust, their troops will yearn for retribution and revolt in battle.

By asking these seven questions, you can determine the winner of any battle, whether it is your own or someone else's.

Listen to and follow my advice, and you will win; you will be a worthy general indeed! However, if you neither listen to nor follow my advice, you will lose; you should not be leading an army! The general who does not take the time to answer the seven questions or even to assess the five factors cannot assess the chances of victory or defeat against the enemy. Generals who do not know how to evaluate their prospects do not know whether they have an advantage or disadvantage compared to their foes or whether they should fight. A leader without a destination in mind will certainly never get there.

- Having paid attention, think outside the box while planning.

- Stay flexible. Circumstances may cause a change in plans.

- Deception is the foundation of all warfare. If your opponent knows everything you will do beforehand, you are doomed to lose. Deception helps you to disguise your schemes and plans, which keeps the opponent guessing.

- You must look unable when you can attack, inactive when activating troops, far away when you are near, and near when you are far away. In this regard, dawdling can often be a wise behavior. Rather than striking right away and being blatant about your intentions, it helps to wait for a little and to appear like nothing is going on when in fact, you are trying to lull the enemy into becoming complacent—and then you strike. Consequently, if your original plans were to wait a while to attack, it helps to look over those plans and ask if attacking now is a wise strategy.

- Tempt the enemy with a gift, then strike when they are vulnerable.

- If your foes have no visible weaknesses, be specially prepared for them. If they are stronger, do not fight. But if you must fight, fight like you have nothing to lose. You will be in a position of inferiority anyway, so use all the resources and manpower at your disposal.

- If your opponents are easily angered, annoy them. If your opponents are humble, try to make them arrogant. For example, if you are an athlete and players on the opposing team complain a lot about their circumstances, find a way to make them mad at you and lose composure. Or, if you are in business and rival companies are quiet about their successes, try to flatter them in the press and make their owners feel cocky about their company's prospects.

- If your opponents are taking their time, hurry them up. If their forces are coordinated, make them disorderly. For example, in basketball, if star players on offense can score regularly on their defenders, the stars' success can force the opposing team to abandon its original defensive strategy and come up with something different. This can hurt the opposing team's players' execution, leaving them vulnerable.

- Attack your rivals where they least expect it and when they least expect it. Keep these tactics secret before you fight.

- Take the time to plan before your battles. No planning is the worst thing you can do, for you have no direction. Little planning is better, but you will still likely lose the battle if you do not take enough time to plot your steps. Taking the time to plan, and crafting a plan based upon your strengths and opportunities, rather than mere chance or luck, is best of all. Knowing that planning is crucial allows you to determine who will likely win or lose.

Chapter Two

Fighting

The point is, ladies and gentlemen, that
greed, for lack of a better word, is good.

—Gordon Gekko

The movie *Wall Street* tells a classic tale of greed, ethics, and business. Regardless of your personal feelings about how Gordon Gekko, played by Michael Douglas, approached his craft and earned his wealth, this chapter and the quote above tackles the idea of increasing your resources. In Gekko's view, greed helped him find resourceful ways to earn money, but in the end, his greed was also his undoing. This chapter is about what happens after fighting a battle and gaining resources. Do not let any profits go to waste. Figure out how they can help you going forward.

In war, every army requires maintenance. Do not raise an army if you cannot pay these costs. There are many costs that one must figure:

- *Financial costs*: How much money will it take? For example, how much money will it take to hire and retain top talent in business?

- *Time costs*: How long will it take to raise an army or achieve the venture? In sports, how long will it take the new coach to turn a losing team into a championship contender?

- *Opportunity costs*: Once you've achieved your goal, what could you have done with the resources you allocated? If you graduated from college or graduate school, how could you have used the time and money you invested in school into either advancing yourself at your current career or pursuing something else?

Try to win as quickly as possible. If winning takes a long time, your weapons won't be as effective, and your troops will suffer in morale. The army will wear down if it tries to attack cities. As a rule of thumb, you should ask yourself, "While I am fighting, how long will it take me to develop a decisive advantage over my opponent?" If you can answer that question, even if you are still fighting, you are much closer to finishing the battle.

For example, in chess, certain tactical maneuvers arise where you can either checkmate the enemy king (win the game) or earn a decisive material advantage (come close to winning). Often, to do so, you must make a move that initially looks bad (for example, giving up a piece or pawn seemingly for nothing) because, in exchange, your opponent has no choice but to play into a sequence of moves resulting in even greater losses.

- If war takes a long time, the state cannot pay the price.

- While you are vulnerable, your enemies will take advantage. Even the wisest sages cannot avoid the inevitable. Thus, while you can lose with short wars, you are unwise to plan for a long one. Long wars never help a country.

- The best generals know the worst war has to offer.

- The best soldiers are efficient in allocating resources.

- In war, bring your weapons from home so that you can fight, but take your food from the enemy. Thus, the army will have enough to eat. In life, make yourself stronger in defeating the enemy. Do not just be satisfied with a victory, but use the resources you have gained in conquest to make your side more profitable.

A country becomes poor when it always has to spend money to send supplies to the enemy. These tributes will ruin the country and its people. Because the army's demand for food is high, its mere presence raises costs in the area. The high cost siphons money away from the locals toward the merchants. When their money is gone, the peasants will suffer from demands that they will not be able to meet. With the loss of strength and money, their homes will be ravaged. Both the peasants and the state will pay the price for lost supplies.

Outside of battle, it is essential to remember that the costs of protracted conflict can affect even those who are not fighting. Keep your battles as short as possible to keep costs down. Hence, the wise general takes supplies from the enemy so that the army's appetite will spare the peasants, thus saving the economy. One unit of local provisions is equivalent to twenty from abroad.

- To kill the enemy, your troops must be aroused to anger.

Find out what motivates your soldiers and what gets under their skin in any field. After that, show them how fighting will help them achieve their objectives.

To gain enemy property, your troops must expect a reward for their conquests. Therefore, in fighting, reward the first fighters who capture resources. Integrate their resources into yours, and make sure that outsiders know that their resources are yours.

- Take good care of captured soldiers. If you do care for them, then they will either turn on you in anger or, if they escape, flee back to their native land. Taking care of your soldiers and consolidating your gains are essential to strengthening yourself when winning battles.

- In war, seek the victory of short and effective battles, not the glory of long campaigns.

- Savvy generals their people's fate and their countries' safety.

Chapter Three

Strategically Attacking

*Baseball is 90 percent mental
and the other half is physical.*

—Yogi Berra

It may be true that many of Yogi Berra's quotes make no sense when you first look at them. But I have often found looking at the deeper meanings behind the quotes and understanding what he is saying to be interesting. Regardless of whether baseball is 50 percent or 90 percent mental, the central idea behind the quote that headlines this chapter is that mental discipline in baseball is the key to success. Consequently, in a chapter about strategic thinking, Yogi Berra's idea fits in in its own quirky, unique way. Or maybe baseball is 90 percent mental, and half of the 10 percent left is physical?

- In practical war, seek to take the enemy's resources, not destroy them.

- True greatness is not in fighting but in winning without fighting.

In disciplines other than armed combat, you want to make gains without starting conflicts or engaging in activities where you are in direct competition with the enemy. Winning via fighting takes bravery, courage, and skill, but winning without fighting takes wisdom and restraint. It is better to plan ahead, so you do not have to put yourself in danger than it is to rush forth impulsively and risk significant loss.

The best defense in war is attacking the enemy strategically; the next best is attacking them politically. The next to worst strategy is to attack enemy soldiers; the worst is to attack enemy supplies. If you attack the enemy's strategy, you can win without fighting, or at minimum, delay fighting. If you stop the enemy through political means, you will have to fight to win, but you can do so without putting your army and resources at risk. If you attack the enemy's forces, you fight with your army, but you could still gain enemy plunder as a prize for victory. But if you attack enemy supplies, even if you win the battle, there is nothing you can gain from your conquest.

The only reason you attack the enemy's resources is if it is a life-or-death matter.

Attacking the enemy's resources takes time, resources, and patience. Impatient generals will attack enemy resources at a cost to themselves and without winning. This is why their plans are foolish.

The best leaders defeat their enemies without fighting at all. They have a gift for seizing the enemies' resources without mounting an attack against them; they topple entire kingdoms without resorting to strategic planning.

> *Example*: When Timex entered the watch industry in the 1950s, the new company decided to challenge the industry giants, the Swiss watchmakers, by producing a low-priced discount watch, which contrasted with the expensive high-quality Swiss watches. As a result, the Swiss did not view Timex watches as a threat to their reputation or to the growth in their industry, which enabled Timex to develop a sustainable competitive advantage without "fighting" the Swiss.

- Aim to capture everything under the sky through better strategy. Then your soldiers will not be exhausted. And your victory will be complete. Winning without fighting is the essence of true strategy.

- If you have superior forces, swarm your opponent. If your forces are equal to your enemy's, try to create a dynamic superiority. Position your army so that you can appear more numerous in places where you can launch an attack. Thus, even though your troops may actually be less in number elsewhere, the opponent cannot exploit your lack of troops where it matters. If slightly inferior, defend yourself. If inferior, flee.

It is a law of war that the strong always beat the weak if they are given enough time.

The general is the first and foremost line of defense for the state. If a general has no weaknesses, the state will be strong. If a general is flawed, the state will be weak.

Generals can make three mistakes that come at the expense of their troops:

1. *Hobbling the army by giving the troops orders they cannot obey.*

   Example: Herbert Sobel led a platoon of Easy Company, a WWII group of paratroopers. Even though he pushed his men very hard, he did not hold himself up to the same standards he expected of others. He was disrespected and lampooned by his men, who bet on which of them would shoot Sobel in combat. He was relieved of his duties before Easy Company went into combat.

2. *Confusing soldiers by giving them orders without knowing their problems.*

   Example: Lieutenant Dike also led an Easy Company platoon, but he often stayed away for long stretches. Since his troops did not respect him, Dike failed miserably when he led into battle and was relieved of his duties.

3. *Instilling fear by giving soldiers orders without being flexible.*

   Example: When managing a group, you must be aware that there is always the very real risk of *groupthink*, where the group is so intimate that its individuals begin to think alike and avoid considering alternative solutions to its problems. Signs of groupthink include peer pressure if any member(s) offer dissenting opinions and the potential for *mindguards*. These people believe their duty is to protect the group against information threatening its viewpoints.

- If the army has low morale, the competition will take advantage. Low morale brings chaos and defeat.

Thus, there are five keys to victory:

1. *Timing your battles*—Learn to pick your battles and when to fight them. Are the circumstances in your favor to fight this battle? For example, as an investor in the stock market, I need to learn the right time to buy and the right time to sell.

2. *Knowing how to handle stronger and weaker forces*—There will be times when your army will be stronger than the opponent's, and there will be times when your army will be weaker. Sooner or later, you will face battles wherein you lack the advantage compared to your opponent, but you will also fight battles from a position of strength. As a chess player, I faced scenarios where I was better, and I was worse, and I had to learn to play with both of these scenarios.

3. *Fostering a sense of unity*—A sense of "togetherness" between the leader and the troops is important. Can the boss communicate and share the company's vision with the employees? Are the athletes on the team all playing with the goal of victory in mind, or do ulterior motives guide them? How much arguing occurs among the team members, and are these disagreements beneficial?

4. *Seizing opportunity*—From time to time, certain opportunities can give you major victories if you seize the moment. For example, when I completed a double major, I had hoped that the additional time and effort spent in college would pay off in greater recognition and higher career pay later in life.

5. *Combining skill with authority*— You need to know what it takes to capitalize on your advantages and the internal fortitude to execute your decision and do it influentially. Leaders with skill but no authority cannot get others to join their cause. Leaders who have authority but no skill waste the talents of their people. The best teams I have been on have had leaders who earned my respect because of what they did and my trust in their leadership.

• Know the enemy and yourself, and you can confidently fight your battles. Know yourself but not your foe, and your chance of winning is halved. Know neither, and you will always lose.

It helps to ask others about your strengths and weaknesses if you want to know yourself. You may be surprised at how much your friends, family, and coworkers know about you that even you do not know about yourself. Also, as you gain experience in battle, you may learn about your tendencies and weaknesses in a battle that can help you.

However, these same principles also apply to learning about your opponent. Ask people who know the enemy about their tendencies; their friends may know even more about them than they do. Also, as time goes on, the enemies' exploits may reveal their strengths and weaknesses as generals.

Chapter Four

It's not the will to win that matters— everyone has that. It's the will to prepare to win that matters.

—Bear Bryant

Every competitor wants to beat their opponent in some way, shape, or form; that is usually why they compete in the first place. However, if merely wanting to win was enough, everyone would have a fair chance of seizing victory.

I chose the quote that opens this chapter by the legendary University of Alabama head coach because the "will to prepare" he talks about is echoed in Sun Tzu's strategies. For example, his emphasis on preparing for good timing or the five guidelines for determining if one should fight can be found at the end of this chapter.

In addition, the will to prepare, in and of itself, is an extension of the will to win. Everyone wants to win, but do you want to win so badly that you are willing to put in the work required beforehand to ensure success?

- The best warriors guaranteed they would not be beaten through good preparation and would defeat the enemy through good timing.

With few, if any, exceptions, people will always have a degree of predictability. We enjoy waking up at the same time each morning, eating the same foods day in and day out, and adopting certain habits in our work and life. Suppose you can tap into something predictable about your opponent, which can potentially work to your advantage. In that case, you can time your attack to respond very well to your opponent's plan.

- The avoidance of defeat is in our control, but only the enemy gives us the chance to win.

- The good fighter can control losing but not victory.

- Just because you *know* how to win doesn't mean you *will* win.

- Not losing shows the enemy that you are defensive, but taking offense implies trying to win.

There is an essential difference between not losing and winning. For you to win, the opponent must also lose. If you are not winning but also not losing, then the opponent is neither winning nor losing. In such a contest, victory and defeat are either present or absent, but one cannot exist without the other.

Being on the defensive shows weakness, and attacking shows strength. The best defensive general hides where they cannot be attacked. The best offensive general attacks from a point where they can attack anyone. Thus, with the former, we can avoid loss; with the latter, we can complete our triumph.

- Greatness is not in seeing victory like others do.

It is not enough to merely look at the results of a contest and conclude that the battle is won. For example, it is not enough for a business executive or stockbroker to look at a company's spike in profits and conclude that the company is winning in the marketplace or for a sports fan to look at the team's success and conclude that the team is starting to win. In both cases, the observer does not see the preparation required to attain observable success.

- Nor is greatness in fighting courageously in battle and receiving praise.

- Obtaining greatness through fighting is like lifting a hair and thinking you have the strength of an ox, seeing the sun and thinking you have the vision of an eagle, or hearing thunder and thinking you have the hearing of a wolf. Even a child can lift a hair from the ground. Those with weak eyesight can still see sunlight because of its brightness. Thunderclaps are so loud that even the hard of hearing can sense a storm approaching.

The best leaders not only win, but they win with great ease. Thus, they aren't recognized for being smart or courageous.

The great general wins without making mistakes. Making no mistakes is important because you beat the enemy when they are already beaten.

The best fighters position themselves not to lose and take advantage of opportunities to defeat the enemy. Thus, the victorious strategist wins first and then fights, while the loser fights first, hoping to win.

The complete leader controls success by virtue of their integrity and discipline.

Successful preparation relies on five things:

1. *Analyzing your battleground*— Study the ground on which you will fight and plan accordingly; even the smallest differences can work to your advantage or disadvantage. For example, a politician running for office needs to know what voters want to be accomplished before campaigning.

2. *Quantifying your resources*— Know the materials you have at your disposal; usually, more supplies are better. For example, a business needs to study its balance sheet and income statements to assess its financial health.

3. *Analyzing your personnel*— Know who will fight with you and your personnel's strengths and weaknesses; the more people and skills at your disposal, the more strength you have relative to your opponent. For example, a sports team needs to assess the strengths and weaknesses of its players compared with those of the opposition.

4. *Estimating your chances*— Determine the likelihood of success or failure of your battle since you do not want to take foolhardy risks. For example, what are the pros and cons if the organization buys a bigger piece of property?

5. *Making a decision*— Finally, judge whether you should go forward with the decision to fight or not; the choice you make has consequences for both you and your opposition. For example, should the army go forth into battle?

Each of these steps depends on the one before it, and the first depends on the terrain on which you'll be doing battle.

- A victorious army is like a pound weighed against a kernel, and a beaten one is like a kernel weighted against a pound.

A superior army rushes forth with all the fury of a tidal wave into a deep gap. This is exercising military might.

Chapter Five

Energy

We have deep depth.

—Yogi Berra

Yes, I led off another chapter with a Yogi Berra quote, and no, I will not quote him a third time later in the book. However, the repetition in "deep depth" really hammers home the wide variety of tactics and strategies available for approaching your planning, almost like a teacher repeatedly bringing up the same concepts in a class. No two people are the same, so no two people will approach the same craft the same way.

- What matters in managing your army is not size but organization. Generals have won battles with small armies and lost battles with enormous ones, but if your army is not organized, it will be prone to chaos and disorder from the outset and doomed to defeat.

- When you are leading your army into battle, the key to victory is not how many troops you have but whether they can communicate effectively with one another.

- The strong beating the weak is like throwing a stone wheel at eggs.

- To defend against any enemy attack, you must know how to use two types of forces—the ordinary and the extraordinary.

Ordinary forces are the resources, personnel, and the like that do not give you an advantage compared to the opposition. Extraordinary forces, on the other hand, give you an advantage. For example, a football team's extraordinary force might be its superstar quarterback or its unbeatable defensive lineup. In contrast, its ordinary force might be the teammates who surround the quarterback or defensive team. For a business, its extraordinary force might be its abundant capital, talented workforce, or its reputation within the industry, while its ordinary force may be other aspects of the company which does not give it an advantage, or maybe even a disadvantage, compared to other companies in the industry.

Use the ordinary to fight but the extraordinary to win. Extraordinary forces are precious; you do not want to risk losing your advantages. Learn to find strategies in which your ordinary force can keep the opponent at bay without putting you at a disadvantage while your extraordinary force constitutes a clear advantage over your opponent's ordinary force. If everything else is roughly equivalent, you can use the advantage of your extraordinary force to win.

- If you learn how to use the extraordinary, you will have an infinite, inexhaustible array of tactics at your disposal.

Knowing only how to use the ordinary force is like painting a picture with only one color on your paintbrush, writing a book with only one letter of the alphabet, or playing music with only one note. Everything looks bland and unimaginative, and there is little to no room for creativity. But learn to use the ordinary and the extraordinary together, and you will be free to scheme schemes, using as much of one and as little of the other as you want. The possibilities are limitless.

Only three primary colors exist—red, yellow, and blue—but they can be combined to form more colors than the human eye could ever see. Seven basic notes—do, re, mi, fa, so, la, and ti—can be combined to form more songs than the human ear could ever hear. Combining five basic tastes—sweet, sour, salty, bitter, and umami—can produce more flavors than the human tongue could ever taste.

In battle, there are two methods of attack—the ordinary and extraordinary—but they can be combined to produce more strategies than the human brain could ever conceive.

The ordinary and the extraordinary give rise to each other, like moving again and again around a circle. As no one can paint all colors, sing all songs, or cook all tastes, so no one can conceive all strategies.

Example: In the 2002 NFL season, former Tampa Bay Buccaneers head coach Jon Gruden held the same position with the Oakland Raiders. When the Buccaneers appeared in the Super Bowl against the Raiders, Gruden used his knowledge of Oakland's offense and personnel to form a game plan against the Raiders. Gruden even played the role of Rich Gannon at practice— taking snaps, throwing passes, and calling plays as if he were the Raiders quarterback. The Bucs had a good team (the "ordinary"), but they also had information (the "extraordinary"). Unsurprisingly, they were dominant in a 48-21 victory over Oakland for their first-ever championship.

Example: Dave Berri, an associate professor of economics at Southern Utah University and the author of *The Wages of Wins: Taking Measure of the Many Myths in Modern Sport*, wrote a post titled "the superstar theory" on his blog, also titled *The Wages of Wins*. The theory's basic premise is that, during the years 1980— 2007, all but two NBA championship teams employed a player who, using Berri's statistical metrics, was approximately three times as productive for his career as an average player. Meanwhile, the Houston Rockets, who won two straight NBA championships in 1994 and 1995, had a star in Hakeem Olajuwon, who was extremely close to this mark. Berri's list included players who played at each of the court's five positions (point guard, shooting guard, small forward, power forward, and center). It also included both players who were well known for scoring the ball and players who were better remembered as top defensive players. Therefore, he theorized that having one or two very good players was necessary as a foundation for a championship team.

As a mighty wave, water can move boulders because of momentum. A falcon can quickly attack and kill its victim because of its timing. Thus, the good fighter will attack like a wave and strike like a falcon.

- Energy is like a crossbow, bent and waiting to strike. Decision is choosing when to release the trigger. Bend your crossbow as far as you can. Do not hesitate to shoot when you sense the opportunity.

- Amid fighting, order may exist despite seeming chaos; amid confusion, your army may appear lost, but it is not losing.

Example: Jack Welch, the former CEO of General Electric, took over General Electric in 1981 amid a time of great corporate upheaval, including corporate restructuring and the PC revolution. Furthermore, he restructured the company through extensive firings, divestitures, and corporate initiatives. However, he helped turn GE into a success story, increasing company value more than thirtyfold and turning out many Fortune 500 CEOs.

- Order, courage, and strength will not last by themselves.

Maintaining order is all about organization; maintaining courage is about energy; maintaining strength is about tactics. Maintaining an army is like maintaining your body It is much better to take simple yet effective measures over time to take care of yourself than to take more invasive, potentially harmful measures to combat the problems resulting from neglect. Just as the body needs food, water, and exercise, an army needs organization, energy, and tactics to function.

- Someone good at keeping the enemy restless offers a gift for them to take, keeping up appearances based on how the enemy responds.

- This person keeps them moving by tempting one's enemy, waiting to strike with the right selection of troops. Do you possess something that is of great value to your opponent? Would giving that possession up for something you value even more be worth it?

- The clever fighter does not ask too much of any one person by picking the right soldiers and using their energy.

- If the right soldiers are put in the right places and given the right amount of work, they can attack as if they are logs or stones. On flat ground, they are motionless but heading down a mountain; they can pick up speed quickly.

The energy from good fighters is like rolling a round stone down a very tall peak. This concludes energy.

Chapter Six

Weak Points and Strong

A good plan implemented today is better than
a perfect plan implemented tomorrow.

—George Patton

The link between the chapter-opening quote and the chapter involves initiative. You must find a balance between the time taken to devise the right plan and the moment you actually implement it often. Even if your plans are not yet perfect, opportunities to gain advantage present themselves. If you are unaware of these moments or try to make everything perfect before taking advantage of them, you risk losing those opportunities.

- Whoever arrives first on the field has time to wait for the enemy; whoever is second will be worn out.

Often in an industry, certain firms are the first in their field to pursue a particular action or establish a position in their market. First movers, as they are called, can take advantage of their timing in several ways:

1. Establishing a reputation for innovation in their industry.

2. Setting a standard for their product or industry that their competitors must copy.

3. Making it more difficult for competitors to gain sales.

4. Having their choice of the best suppliers to make their product.

5. Potentially establishing a strong financial position soon after pursuing the action.

6. The clever fighter takes the initiative but does not give it to the enemy.

A clever fighter can coax foes out of hiding by offering them an edge or keeping them from getting closer by attacking their army and imposing losses upon them.

If enemies are in no hurry, they can be hurried; if well fed, they can be starved; if still, they can be made to move around.

Example: In the 1960s, Lee Iacocca convinced executives at Ford to produce a car that he envisioned would cater to the Baby Boomer demographic that was set to explode. The Ford Motor Company Mustang stormed the car market and stunned rivals from the outset. It generated $1.1 billion in profit in its first two years, which was especially impressive in the 1960s.

Example: The 1998 Denver Broncos scored a lot of points and scored them early; in the first quarter of their games that season, Denver scored 144 points while allowing only 54 to their opponents. The Broncos' initiative in scoring helped them win their first thirteen regular season games, finish with a 14-2 record, and win their second consecutive Super Bowl.

- Make your enemy respond quickly to your threat; attack where the enemy least expects it.

An army can travel a long way without problems if it doesn't march in enemy territory.

You can succeed on offense if you attack what can't be defended and on defense if you defend what can't be attacked.

Example: Many businesses employ a "focus" strategy, focusing only on specific types of customers or products. They can hold their own against larger businesses with a more global reach because they have developed a following in their market that would take bigger corporations a significant amount of time, money, and effort to reproduce.

- The skillful general leaves the opponent at a loss on how to respond.

- Oh, art of secrecy! Through you, we can't be seen or heard and control our enemy's destiny!

- You can't be stopped if you attack enemies where they are weak; you can be safe if you are faster than your opponents.

- If you want to draw enemies out from shelter, all you have to do is attack a place that they have to protect.

Example: Harley-Davidson motor-cycles are uniquely American, and as could be expected, the company has always had a very strong base in the United States, But in the early 1980s, foreign competitors were able to make inroads on Harley's turf and were able to attack the very market that they needed to defend by importing and selling motorcycles at a very low price. The resulting competition put Harley under tremendous pressure to survive, and the U.S. government intervened by imposing taxes on imported motorcycles. Fortunately, the company navigated through the recession and even asked the government to lift the tariffs a year before they were set to expire.

- If you don't want to fight when you are vulnerable, you just need to keep enemies from going where they want.

By learning enemies' habits while staying undercover, you can concentrate your forces while theirs are divided. You can create a dynamic superiority wherever you attack.

If the enemies strengthen one side, attack the other. If they strengthen themselves everywhere, they are strong nowhere. The enemy only has a limited supply of resources with which they can strengthen themselves. If they try to strengthen themselves everywhere, they are spread thin because they have to allocate the same amount of resources to many more points. Thus, it is easier to attack them at any point because they do not have many troops defending that point.

- Whoever has the initiative can concentrate forces at a point of attack, often leading to a numerical advantage.

- If you know when to fight, you can concentrate forces regardless of distance.

- If you can attack the inferior with the superior, your foe is in trouble.

- You must keep your place of attack secret. The more spots the enemy has to guard, the better.

By knowing when and where to fight, you can concentrate your forces. If you don't know the time or place of the coming battle, one side of your attack cannot support the other. How much more so if these sides are far apart!

Although an enemy may have more soldiers, you can stop them from fighting. If you can figure out what they are planning and where they are strong and where they are weak, you can find ways to attack them, to interfere with their plans. By forcing them to react, you can keep them from retaliating and using their advantage in personnel.

> *Example*: In the 1920s, Ford Motor Company was a dominant player in the automotive industry. By mass-producing a limited variety of models, owning and producing its supplies (backward integration), and keeping model changes to a minimum, Ford could sell cars at low prices that competitors could not match.
>
> However, as customers were shopping for a second car, they were willing to pay extra for cars with additional options. General Motors responded by providing a lineup of more expensive models with

what customers were looking for. Despite Ford's cost advantages, the sheer cost of adjusting its low-price strategy kept them from responding to GM's threat.

- Disturb the enemy; find out why they are active or inactive.

- Draw enemies out to find where they are in danger. Examine them, and you will find out where they are strong and where they are weak.

- The best way to strike is to keep your tactics secret. Conceal them, and even the sneakiest spies and wisest minds cannot plan against you.

- Flexible plans ensure victory.

The importance of flexibility is what most people do not understand. If your plans are flexible, you do not need to rely on a specific course of action in order to succeed. Your odds of success improve when you account for multiple scenarios because, things frequently force you to change your plans anyway.

Everyone can understand how tactics help you win, but not everyone can understand the preparation winning takes.

Change your tactics depending on your circumstances. What worked once may not work again. For example, I am learning about the value of marketing via the Internet and social networking pages. Ten, or maybe even five, years ago, many marketers did not use Facebook, Twitter, Instagram, or TikTok. Twenty years ago, the Internet was not as widespread as it is now. The technology behind media is always evolving, becoming more advanced so as businesses and businesspeople seek to sell their products, the complexity and variety of mediums they use to sell their products change.

Military tactics are like water; they escape the high places and rush down. Water flows where the ground tells it to go; the soldier plans his victory according to his foe. Thus, as water changes its shape, warfare changes its conditions.

- Those who adapt and, thus, win deserve high praise indeed.

In nature, everything is evolving. None of the elements remain predominant; each season makes way for the next; the days change in length; the moon goes through its cycle. Similarly, in battle, no tactical or strategic style is predominant. The nature of warfare in any discipline is constantly evolving. As with the moon, a style becomes popular; then it fades into obscurity before it becomes popular again. The best generals learn to live with and embrace change.

Chapter Seven

Maneuvering

He knew that the path to winning is sometimes a winding one. He understood that managing less was managing more, that the key to success was producing more with less. And he knew that he had to manage many businesses while imposing a single vision.

—Jeffrey Krames on Jack Welch, former CEO of General Electric and columnist for *Bloomberg Businessweek*

Imagine that you are hiking on a mountain trail and trying to reach your destination. Instinctively, you know that the shortest distance from where you start to where you finish is a straight line. Unfortunately, going in a straight line means having to cross a forest thick with trees, climb right through a mountain path, or swim across a tumultuous ocean. However, by taking a paved path and a longer route, you can save yourself a ton of hassles and arrive at your destination in a shorter time than you could ever manage by taking the direct route.

Often, the same advice applies if you are trying to defeat an opponent or achieve a goal. The longest way around really could be the shortest path to success.

- In war, generals get orders from their bosses.

- Having built and readied their armies, the generals must now position their soldiers for success in battle.

- The toughest part of maneuvering is making the long, winding road the shortest, quickest path to success and turning your weaknesses into strengths.

- Thus, despite a slower start and a longer path, arriving at your destination after fooling the enemy is a sign of knowing the ruse of deviation.

    Example: The Japanese seized control of the video recorder industry by selling their products at a loss for the first year, anticipating that prices for producing recorders would go down, resulting in profits within five years. Japanese companies earned a competitive advantage in the market by thinking forward to the next five years rather than only the next year as American companies did.

- When you maneuver well, your maneuvers will succeed beautifully. When you execute strategies improperly, they will fail miserably.

- Strike a balance between preparing for the battle and getting there on time.

- Do not befriend people if you don't know their motives. Ask them why they want to join you, but also pay attention to what they don't say. Are they easygoing or standoffish, confident or humble, friendly or aloof? When in doubt, trust your instincts about the person.

- Know your battleground before you fight.

In battle, seek advice from people who know your terrain better than you do. In life, seek advice from people more experienced in your field than you. Often, by learning from the successes and failures of others, you can gain a lot of valuable experience that would take you months, even years, to learn from your successes and failures. By learning from veterans' experiences in your field, you can expand your knowledge.

- In war, you will succeed if you successfully conceal your plans or send misleading signals, but be wary of fighting using underhanded tactics. People who "play dirty" often fight out of fear, not skill.

- Time your attack and change your methods as the situation demands.

When you are attacking, attack with the force of a mighty gale. When marching, be as majestic as a forest. When taking supplies, devour them like a mighty blaze. When standing, stand like a mighty summit. When hiding, hide the mystery of things behind the clouds. When you move, move with the speed of a lightning strike. When you plunder the countryside, share the bounty with your troops so they may be motivated.

Take the time to think about the consequences before you act. Before you act, ask yourself, if you make the decision, what would be the best-case scenario and what would be the worst-case scenario? If you feel that the consequences of the worst-case scenario, combined with the chances that the worst-case scenario comes to fruition, outweigh the benefits and chances of the best-case scenario, then do not make the decision. Also, remember that not making a decision is, in itself, a decision.

- Victory goes to those who know deception. This is how you maneuver.

- Use the appropriate method of communication depending upon the circumstances. What works at one time may not work at another.

Communication should foster a spirit of unity. Everybody should move at the same pace, no one advancing too far ahead or lurking too far behind. This is how you lead a large army.

Sometimes, people lose heart, whether individually (commanders) or in groups (armies).

Usually, people will be energetic and in high spirits at the beginning of a day or campaign. But as the day progresses or the campaign draws on, they will become more dispirited and less energetic.

Watch out for low morale in your army, but attack your enemies when they are downtrodden and want to go home. This is psychology. In life, if you sense that a team's mood is down or that a business is reeling, and people feel dispirited, or that your adversary is facing hardship, take advantage of their troubles and strike them while they're down. But watch out if your team feels dispirited because you are particularly vulnerable to an enemy attack.

- Good generals are organized when they battle a disorderly enemy and serene when the enemy is panicking and reckless. This is how you maintain self-control.

- They are close to the battle when waiting for a faraway enemy, rested when awaiting a tired one, and well fed when awaiting a hungry one. This is self-discipline.

To make this work, do not wait for the enemy to be far away, worn out, or hungry. Instead, take the time to make sure your men are close, rested, and well-fed so that when your opponent arrives, you can attack while your opponent's troops are down. Also, by having the discipline to keep your army close to the battle, well fed, and rested, you guard against becoming far away, hungry, or exhausted—the risk of being attacked while you are down.

- Good generals don't attack an army when coordinated and in high spirits. Instead, by being proactive in their preparation and finding out what motivates their troops, good generals attack when their armies are coordinated and in high spirits. This is adaptation.

Do not attack where the enemy is strong. This is common sense.

Do not react to enemy deception; do not attack soldiers who have a sense of detecting danger.

Do not attack an army in high spirits after a conquest.

When attacking a desperate opponent, stay calm and give yourself room to retreat if things go wrong.

This is warfare as an art form.

Chapter Eight

Varying Tactics

Nearly all men can stand adversity, but if you want to test a man's character, give him power.

—Abraham Lincoln

People can be remarkably resilient in the face of tragedy. All of us are bound to face great adversity at one point or another.

However, power and prosperity are tests all their own. The ability to do the right thing when nothing else is prompting you, or even when no one else is prompting you, is truly commendable. It's one thing to want to feel appreciated as a follower, but as a leader, do you treat others the way you want them to treat you? You may believe intellectually that all people deserve respect, but do you treat your mailman with the same respect you would give to a boss or colleague? Indeed, this chapter covers some of the trials of leadership.

- In battle, the superior orders the general, who readies the army to fight.

- Don't put yourself into needlessly difficult situations. If you do, be prepared to scheme or fight your way out of trouble. Seek help from friends who can easily help you.

It's just as important to know what not to do as it is to know what to do.

> *Example*: As previously discussed, certain tactical maneuvers in chess arise that allow you to either checkmate the enemy king or win a lot of material. If you do not take advantage of these opportunities, the opponent may notice an overlooked tactic and make a move that takes it away, making the game that much longer and putting you at a greater risk of drawing or losing.

- Generals who know how to do things right and do them differently depending upon the circumstances are of high caliber.

For a general, no amount of knowledge about the terrain will result in victory if it is not accompanied by a willingness to change plans as necessary.

- Wise leaders know their areas of strength and weakness.

Wise leaders know how to win their battles by knowing their strengths. They can minimize their losses by knowing where they are weak.

When you are leading, annoy enemy commanders. Strike them where they are weak, irritate them, make them worry, tempt them with gifts, and keep them moving.

Err on the side of caution. Always plan as if the opponent is about to strike you regardless of the situation, and respond accordingly. However, if you sense that you have an opportunity to strike your opponent and you have the means to do it quickly and without occurring great losses, then you must do so. In battle, it is important not to be foolhardy and rush into an attack, But it is also important to take the initiative when the situation calls for it.

Be wary of the following five traits, each of which can lead to defeat:

1. *Recklessness* destroys you with a lack of restraint.

2. *Fearfulness* subdues you with lack of bravery.

3. *Irritability* humiliates you with the urge to lose your composure.

4. *Sensitivity* shames you with a need for honor.

5. *Excessive altruism* troubles you with neglecting your own needs.

These faults will cause any general to fall in war. When the army falls apart, look for these traits in the leader. Ponder them.

Chapter Nine

The Marching Army

*People won't go along with you if they
can't get along with you.*

—John Maxwell

Have you ever had to work for a boss or a supervisor that you couldn't get along with? At best, it's a minor nuisance to a career and a line of work that you find satisfying. At worst, it's a symptom of major leadership problems that can tear your team apart.

- If you are a leader, chances are good that you will have to lead and learn from your people. You will need to lead them with a unified vision, but you also need them to trust and respect you. A leader who puts both qualities together has the potential to achieve many great things.

- When the army is on the battleground and observing the opposition, it should seek favorable terrain. If the opposing forces have a favorable position, the army should not try to fight them there.

Example: During the American Civil War, the town of Gettysburg, Pennsylvania, was potentially "favorable terrain" for both sides. Several roads met at this location, making it a key hub for moving armies. Furthermore, it was surrounded by various hills and heights that offered an advantage in the battleground for either army, including Seminary Ridge to the west and Cemetery Ridge to the South. The Union army occupied Gettysburg in preparation for a Confederate attack. Over three days, the Confederates tried to attack the Union from a disadvantage in terrain, but to no avail. The consequences were significant: The North was able to stem the tide of a great invasion from the South.

If your opponents are on a battleground that is unfavorable to you, do not try to fight them at that battleground. Leverage an advantage in the battleground and time your attack.

If you dislike the battleground you are on, get out of it as soon as possible. Change the conditions so you can get an advantage.

In battle, if neither side has an apparent advantage in the battleground, look for the tiniest advantages you can find in this area. In life, if you and your opponent are fighting on apparently equal terms, keep your eyes and ears open for any tiny advantages that you can gain. For example, in chess, even if both sides have the same number of pieces and pawns, have their pieces positioned in identical ways, and the features of the position on the chessboard do not benefit either side, one side always gets to move next, while the other has to wait. In many cases, the side that gets to move can favorably use the advantage in time.

Learning how to assess your battleground and reacting accordingly can help you fight on any terrain.

Every team wants to have an advantage in the battleground. Things will go well for an army with an advantage in a battleground, which will help the army win.

When you find great terrain, position yourself to get the most out of it. If you position yourself on great terrain, you will act in the best interests of your army.

If you have to cross perilous ground, wait until the worst is over if you are able.

There are some highly disadvantageous places where no army must ever fight. However, you must try and get the enemy to go close to these places, giving you an advantage in battleground.

Watch out for traps close to your battleground. Be wary; if something looks too good to be true, it probably is. If something looks out of place in the battleground, it may clue you in that something is not right.

Lastly, determine how your situation changes if you seize upon what looks to be an advantage.

Learn to analyze your opponent and your territory. Even the tiniest details can clue you in on what to watch for.

In battle, strength in numbers is only useful if you take your time to plan and don't act impulsively. Beware of underestimating your adversary.

- Your troops won't recognize tough love unless they know it is out of love.

- Discipline before attachment breeds disobedience. Attachment without discipline breeds entitlement.

If you want to avoid entitlement and disobedience, first give your people time to grow accustomed to you and your method of leadership. Think of a mother caring for her baby, giving the child time to grow attached to her. The mother does not discipline the child until the two of them have had time to develop a bond together. In the same way, take the time to develop relationships with your team members before you start administering discipline when they step out of line. Do both of these steps, and do them in order, and you are well on your way to making your team a well-disciplined, well-coached unit.

Thus, you must first show compassion for your troops and then restrain them with discipline. This is a certain way to win.

If your troops are accustomed to obeying orders before battle, they will be disciplined during battle. If your troops are not accustomed to obeying orders, however, then they will not be disciplined during battle.

If leaders believe in their people but ask for obedience, both parties will benefit.

Chapter Ten

Battleground

Coaching is nothing more than eliminating mistakes before you get fired.

—Lou Holtz

This chapter is all about mistakes. Perfection in any discipline is not easy to attain if it can be attained at all. However, it is the standard we should strive for to become excellent in any field. Everyone is vulnerable to making mistakes. However, making the same mistakes over and over, in particular, can often spell trouble for an army, a team, or a business. The important thing is that you learn from your mistakes and correct them before they doom your team.

Several different types of battleground exist.

Battleground types include:

1. *A battleground on which both sides can readily move*—If you are required to face your opponent on this type of battleground, seek any advantage in

the battleground that you can get and keep yourself supplied. Thus, you can fight with an advantage.

2. *A battleground you can leave but have trouble reentering*—In battle, this could be an island surrounded by tumultuous waters or a country that blocks entry to most outsiders. In business, it could be the industry that requires significant startup costs or the company that has built up a reputation of trust over a long period. In each case, leaving the industry or sully the reputation is easy, but it is hard to get it back. The amount of trouble you have in reentering depends upon your enemy. You can beat an unprepared foe, but if they are prepared, watch out.

3. *A battleground disadvantageous for either side*—For example, any industry in danger of becoming obsolete soon. Do not take any bait that enemies may offer you. However, if you can maneuver in a way that allows you to get the enemies partially inside, then you can strike them when they are at a disadvantage.

4. *A protracting battleground*—Taking the initiative is not an advantage on this battleground. Often, you are in a situation where you are not at an advantage by trying to move first, and you are not at a disadvantage by delaying a strike. A perfect example in chess is a "closed game," where pieces often cannot move freely, and where taking your time before attacking is preferable, as it gives you

time to strengthen your position. This strategy is wise in other disciplines where time is not of the essence. Use your time wisely and prepare your army for an attack. See if you can bait the enemy into becoming vulnerable; then, you can attack favorably. But see that you are not yourself baited.

5. *A battleground through which only one army can travel at a time*—If you are here, prepare for your opponent and lie in wait. If your opponent is in this terrain, wait until they are unprepared before attacking.

6. *A battleground that can confer a tremendous advantage*—If you are on this terrain, look to take the most favorable position and wait for your opponent to attack you. If your opponent is here, try to coax them away, but do not fight them when they are in a position of strength.

   Example: A business that seeks to attack an industry leader should not try to completely mimic the leader's original strategy to gain market share (to fight where the leader has an advantage). If a new competitor attempts this strategy, the leader can use its advantages to retaliate against the competitor and exhaust the competitor's lesser resources. Rather, the competitor should try and focus on employing a different strategy that only partly copies the leader's strategy and advantages but, at its core, seeks to gain share through different means entirely. For example, if the leader is a low-cost firm, rather than market low-cost products, the competitor could attack with premium products with prices that are not exorbitant but not too low in price.

If the sides cannot readily attack each other, starting a fight won't be easy and will not be to your advantage.

These are the six types of ground. Every general must study these different types of terrain and the advantages and disadvantages of each.

Six troubles can befall an army.

1. All else equal, a far inferior force will *flee* against a far superior one.

2. If soldiers have too much power, there is *revolt*.

3. If officers have too much power, there is *tyranny*.

4. When officers and soldiers are neurotic and fight out of a sense of bitterness, there is *rage*.

5. When the general is neither a good leader nor an effective communicator, the troops are disorganized, resulting in *anarchy*.

6. When the general cannot judge the army's chances for victory and does not put the right people in the right places, there is a *rout*.

The battleground is a soldier's best friend, but planning and leadership define the general.

Every general should know about the six troubles, for each can court disaster.

Only the person who knows these things *and* can put them into good use will win the battle.

Trust your gut. If you know you will win the fight or if you know you will lose, then you must fight or not fight, regardless of criticism.

The general who sacrifices personal gain for the good of the army is a highly valued asset.

Treat your soldiers like family, and they will do anything for you. In a family, people laugh together, cry together, and enjoy each other's company. Take time to be with your soldiers and listen to what they say. All people deserve to be treated with this dignity and respect, but those under your command—whether they are your children, your subordinates, or your sales reps—need this treatment even more.

If you do not discipline your soldiers, they will be insubordinate.

If you know your enemy and yourself, you have the foundation for victory. If you know your battleground and circumstances, you can make your victory complete.

Chapter Eleven

The Nine Types of Turf

Winning is not everything—
but making the effort to win is.

—Vince Lombardi

According to the cliche, when the going gets tough, the tough get going. But often, you hear people who say that, even though they won a game or a race, they weren't satisfied with their performance in victory, or they are criticized for lack of effort. Can a team spur forth the same effort against an "easy" game that they would exert in a difficult situation? What if victories and losses are not just on the line in each contest? What if we recognized that the preparation and discipline we exert in "meaningless" games would show itself in those contests where everything is on the line? What if we didn't need last-ditch situations to jolt ourselves into working hard at every game?

Battleground describes the comprehensive sum of territory over which you are fighting, while *land* describes individual features and segments of a battleground or the components.

There are several types of land:

1. A battle fought on your *homeland* is one in which generals fight on their turf. For example, a company's homeland could be its "home market," where it first started, and where its business may be strongest.

2. *Short-range land* is a short distance into enemy territory. For example, a company could enter a new industry without extensive startup costs. Keep moving in short-range land.

3. *Crucial land* can give either side an edge. For example, in politics, crucial land is the "swing vote" that could be the key to either candidate's victory. In business, crucial land could be that key demographic that two or more industry competitors are fighting over, knowing that if they gain a stronghold in that segment, they will have more market share. Don't fight an opponent who is on crucial land.

4. Either army can move easily on *open land*. For example, this could be a startup company that can afford to make quick tactical or strategic moves in the industry because of its small size. Stay together on open land. Since both armies can move easily here, if you are not together, the opponent can easily move in and disrupt your forces, throwing you into disarray.

5. You can easily get help from your neighbors in *reinforcing land*. For example, teammates on a motorsports team could share information about their cars to help them go faster. On reinforcing land, join together with your friends.

6. *Long-range land* is deeper into enemy territory than short-range land. For example, this could be a company entering an industry with high startup costs. Gather up plunder in long-range land.

7. *Non-open land*, unlike open land, makes it difficult for an army to move. For example, in chess, this is where there are not a lot of open lines for attack. Keep moving in non-open land.

8. It is difficult to escape *dead-end land*. An example of dead-end land in business is an industry where the costs of leaving are very high, be it financial, emotional, strategic, or legal. Plan your way out of dead-end land.

9. Fighting and dying are your only two options in *survival land*. A sports team facing a huge deficit on the scoreboard is in survival land. A business deep in debt and not making profits is also on survival land. In these desperate situations, if you do nothing, your situation's danger will only get worse before it overwhelms you. That is why you must do something to turn the tide, or it will all be over for you and your army. Fight on survival land.

Every general must get to know these types of land well.

- Skilled fighters keep the enemy army uncoordinated. They advance only when they have the advantage. When they don't have an advantage, they halt.

If enemies are coordinated and ready to strike, take something they want, and they will do anything to get it back. People value certain things very highly, even higher than victory. If you can take something your enemies want, they may be able to beat you, but it will come at the price of the thing they treasure even more.

For example, I have negotiated lower prices for certain goods or services by threatening to walk away. Even if the salespeople "win" the argument that their product is worth the original price, they will lose the sale and the money I would have paid. Thus, it is possible in some cases to get a lower price, and both of us can win the deal.

- In war, speed is key. Attack your enemies when and where they least expect it.

The following are general principles for an army:

- The tougher the challenge, the greater the teamwork among your troops.

- Plan to keep yourself well supplied on your journey.

- Take care of your soldiers. Don't take energy and strength for granted. Keep moving, and devise deep strategic plans.

- Put your troops into a desperate situation, and they will rather die than quit. In the face of death, they may achieve the unthinkable and give all their effort.

- Soldiers with nothing to lose have nothing to fear. They will stand firm and fight if they are deep in an enemy country with no escape or no aid. Thus they will stay alert and dependable and do your will without being asked.

- Prohibit any mention of good or bad luck, and your troops will not fear death. If you believe in superstition, you believe that you do not control your destiny; wins and losses will not be chalked up to differences in planning, strategy, or tactics but to the fickle nature of luck.

- If your soldiers aren't worried about money, it is not because they loathe it. If they don't expect to live long, it is not because they don't want to.

- Come the day of battle, your troops may cry or pee their pants. But throw them into a desperate situation, and they will show legendary courage. In other words, the worse your situation appears to be, and the greater the challenge the team faces, the harder the team will perform. People play like there is nothing to lose because the consequences of loss are so great.

Example: Southwest Airlines faced massive obstacles when the company was founded in 1967. During the company's infancy, three other airlines tried to put it out of business, but Herb Kelleher spearheaded the legal battles to ensure its survival and eventually won in the Texas Supreme Court. When the company sold one of four planes to generate cash, Southwest miraculously figured out a way to keep up all of its flights on its three remaining planes. Southwest Airlines' business strategists even pioneered peak and off-peak pricing when the company could not fill its planes. As a result, the company succeeded in the face of incredible pressure, increasing its total assets more than six hundred times from 1971 to 2006.

- Troops under a skilled army are like the Shuai Ran, a snake found in the Chung Mountains. Strike it at one end, and it will strike you with the other. Strike in the middle, and it will strike at both ends.

Can an army coordinate itself like the Shuai Ran? Yes, it can! Even though the people of Wu and the people of Yueh are enemies, if they are in dire straits, they will help each other like the left-hand helps the right. Regardless of your discipline, it might be appropriate to enlist the help of an opponent if both you and your adversary are facing great danger and you need each other's capabilities to fend it off or if both of you are fighting an opponent who is willing to take and capable of taking both of you down.

Do not just rely on your supplies.

1. The principle of army management is to set up a universal standard of courage. Hence, the wise general leads an army as if it were one person.

2. A general's job is to keep quiet and lay down the law.

Generals should not tell their soldiers the strategy they're planning until the time is right.

By changing strategies, generals keep the enemy guessing. They keep the enemy from knowing their plans by moving and taking the long route.

At the key moment, the general who has secretly developed a new strategy kicks the ladder away from soldiers climbing up a distance.

They drive their soldiers like shepherds herd their sheep. Even the sheep don't know where the shepherds will go next.

- The general's business is to organize their host and bring them through danger.

Generals must learn the different measures associated with different lands; they must study the nuances associated with each type of turf, the suitability of different tactics, and human nature.

- When invading an enemy country, the deeper the penetration, the greater the teamwork.

- When your enemy is behind you and a small path is ahead, you are on dead-end land. When there is nowhere to hide, you're on survival land.

- On your homeland, unite your forces.

- On short-range land, keep your army close together.

- On critical land, hurry up your rear.

- On open land, pay attention to defense.

- On reinforcing land, unite with your friends.

- On long-range land, keep yourself well supplied.

- On non-open land, keep on moving.

- On dead-end land, block all escape.

- On survival land, tell your soldiers they are as good as dead. Soldiers are inclined to give their all when there is no choice but to win.

Example: Many successful entrepreneurs are successful partly because they know their reputations and their livelihoods are at stake every time they make a sale. For them, failure is not an option because they know that the consequences of failure are too great. Their attitude gives them an edge in business.

A general who always ignores the signs of a battleground will never become great.

When a great army attacks a mighty state, it disrupts the coordination of the enemy army. It intimidates the enemy and prevents allies from helping.

To beat an enemy, you don't have to join with other states, but you can beat them with your secret plans.

Reward your soldiers on merit, not tradition or seniority, and you can lead an army as one.

The best sports teams reward their best performers with the biggest contracts. In chess, the best players get named grandmasters. In everyday life, you may have to change your policies about rewards and/or go from giving rewards based on experience to rewards based on merit. Doing so may offend the more experienced, but more importantly, it will help you keep your top talent.

Get your soldiers into a position where victory is the only option, but do not tell them why you are putting them into that position.

Put your army in a position where it must succeed, and it will survive. That said, survival is much easier if you have put yourself into an advantageous position than if you are fighting from inferiority. Fight from inferiority, and you will likely survive, but fight from ahead, and you will likely win.

It is when things look bad when the army can do much good.

Success in warfare lies in adapting to your opponent.

By keeping on the enemy's tail, we can overthrow its leader. In achieving the goal of victory through indirect means, you can accomplish something by being crafty.

Do not allow enemy spies to enter your camp when you first take control. Then, your plans will remain secret.

In life, be wary of people who look like they want to help your cause but only mean to do you harm. Be skeptical if someone you don't know wants to help you. Question their motives. Be choosy in selecting the people who you allow to help you. When in doubt, trust your instincts.

Take advantage of any opportunities the enemy gives you.

Delay your enemies by taking something they want, and wait for their arrival.

Adapt to the enemy until you can fight a winning battle.

At first, look quiet and reserved; then, when the enemy gives you a chance, don't delay in striking, and it will be too late for your enemy to stop you.

---◇◆◇---

Chapter Twelve

---◇◆◇---

Attack with Fire

If everything seems under control,
you're not going fast enough.

—Mario Andretti

Mario Andretti's quote relates to the idea of control. Sometimes, to be the fastest driver or to win, it is not enough to be "in control"—to be content planning, scheming, and attacking like normal. In these situations, you need to bring something entirely different into your strategy that the opponent is not expecting. That something may be the ambitious sacrifice of material in chess, the audacious new business plan, or the trick play in sports. Taking the right risks at the right times can help you win. In "giving up control," you gain the speed or the edge to win.

You can attack with fire in several different ways, by burning soldiers, supplies, incoming trains, weapons, and paths.

Every fire needs both a medium and materials to ignite.

There are proper days and proper times to attack with fire. Wait for a dry season when the stars have aligned, for there are likely to be strong winds.

Example: At the end of the 1996 NFL season, the Green Bay Packers played in Super Bowl XXXI against the New England Patriots. While watching football on television before the game, Packers quarterback Brett Favre noticed that the winning team ran a play already in Green Bay's playbook, resulting in a long pass and a touchdown.

While playing in the actual game, Favre noticed that the Patriots came out in a defense similar to the one he'd seen on TV. He called the same play he saw earlier in the day; it worked to perfection, resulting in a Green Bay score that contributed to a 35-21 Packers victory and a championship. Favre made a play that helped out his team immensely in making a risky but unexpected and powerful tactic.

In attacking with fire, there are several principles you must follow:

- When fire breaks out inside the enemy camp, attack from outside.

- If rival soldiers do not shriek or scatter, take your time. Attack when the flames are at their highest if you can. If not, keep your ground.

- Don't wait for a fire to start inside if you can attack with fire from outside.

- When you start a fire, don't attack in the direction it's moving.

- Wait for the dark of the night to start a fire when the wind has died down.

- The army must know how and when to attack with fire.

- Attacking with fire shows brains; attacking with water shows brawn. Attacking with fire can defeat enemies, but it will also destroy their resources, and you will not be able to consolidate your gains. However, attacking with water can hinder enemies' paths without destroying their resources, so you can still become stronger in defeating those enemies.

- Make your gains work for you. Not doing so is wasteful.

- The wise ruler plans ahead; the wise general develops resources.

- Only fight battles when you can win, or you are in trouble.

- Rulers and generals should fight because doing so are to their advantage, not out of anger. Generals who fight out of anger fight merely to satisfy their vengeance and rage, not because they believe they have an advantage.

- Moods can change for the better, but kingdoms that fall can't rise again, and people who die can't live again. Thus, the wise ruler is sensible, the wise general cautious. This keeps kingdoms and armies intact.

Chapter Thirteen

Spying

*I have always hated that damn James
Bond. I'd like to kill him.*

—Sean Connery

Ironically, this chapter's opening quote from an actor
famous for playing James Bond in movies breaks from
the other quotes in the earlier chapters. Rather than
provide a serious look into the nature of competition, it is
meant to be a more humorous take on the chapter's topic.
Through characters like Bond, Hollywood portrays spies
in a political context; spies in movies learn secrets and
stop evil schemes that can topple entire countries and
governments. However, it is possible to employ spies in
other contexts as well. Even without fighting in battle or
leading an army, spies can make all the difference between
victory and defeat.

Raising an army costs the state and starts rumors of
war at home and away. Soldiers will grow weary from
exhaustion, and families will have difficulty maintaining
their work.

Hostile armies may fight each other for years to gain one victory, so a leader who is not willing to pay the price knows the enemy is cruel indeed. Such a leader is not a true general, a true ruler, or a true winner.

Prior knowledge enables the wise monarch and good commander to achieve the extraordinary.

This foreknowledge cannot come from superstition, intuition, or deduction. It must be obtained from those who know the enemy.

Hence, there are several types of spies.

1. We hire natives from enemy locals.

2. We hire traitors from enemy officers.

3. We hire converts from enemy spies.

4. We give deceivers rumors to share with the enemy.

5. When survivors bring news from the enemy camp.

When the five types work in harmony and in secret, the way they work together is beautifully complex and invaluable to any sovereign.

Of all your men, keep your spies closest, reward them the most, and keep them the most secretive.

For example, a business can hire an executive with inside knowledge of an industry competitor, or a sports team can hire a coach who has experience with the team's rival. Make sure you treat spies well, and they will reward you with valuable information.

Only the wise can hire spies.

Only the compassionate and unselfish can use spies, whether they are your own or were converted from the enemy.

If you cannot be kind to the spies you capture, they will run away from you, taking all their valuable secrets with them. Worse, you risk your spies running away and giving valuable information to the other army.

The blatant and brash cannot get information from spies.

Remember, all warfare is based on deception. If you make no attempt to conceal your plans, the enemy will know you have learned something, and the information that you have learned will be useless.

Watch out, take care, and use your spies for everything!

A spy who says too much too soon should be punished, along with any accomplices. Spies who say too much could share your secrets with both the accomplice and the enemy, putting you and your army in great danger.

Regardless of the objective, use your spies to find out the names of key personnel of the enemy.

Enemy spies must become converts.

You can use information gained from enemy spies to hire natives and traitors. You can also use this information to help deceivers spread rumors. Lastly, you can use converts to employ surviving spies at the right time.

You use spies to know the enemy, and it all begins with converts. Treat your converts well.

In ancient times, a spy helped the Shang Dynasty rise to power, and a spy helped the dynasty after that conquer the Shang. This shows that only the insightful ruler and the wise general can use the smartest people as spies and achieve the extraordinary.

Spying is crucial; the army depends on spies when deciding what to do.

Conclusion

I hope this book has taught you a lot about how to apply the principles from *The Art of War* to your craft or your life. Going through the process of writing *The Art of War Simplified* has taught me a lot. Thinking about how to write Sun Tzu's principles in a form that is easier to read and looking for examples and explanations that capture the spirit of these principles has helped enrich my understanding of the original book in a way simply reading it did not.

Even after going through the text of this book, you may still find yourself somewhat confused or intimidated by all of the military talk. That is fine. Again, the first time I read the original, it did not make sense to me either. In fact, it took me almost seven years from the time I first read *The Art of War* to read it again and gain a better understanding of the concepts.

Another piece of advice, especially for first-time readers, is to focus less on Sun Tzu's sayings and more on the overall concepts he is teaching. This will enable you to stop worrying about how to apply specific sayings to your situation while still receiving valuable lessons.

I have found opportunities to tap into the principles in this book, which have enriched my life, partly because I have included examples from my own experience in the main text.

As an author, I do not feel that it is fair to ask you, the reader, to embrace and apply the pointers I am writing about if I do not hold myself to the same principles. Thus, I conclude with two final examples from my experience with these principles to show how using this knowledge has helped me.

First, this book was the realization of a personal goal of mine since my first year of college. Ironically, it was meant as more of an exercise in building my personal branding when I initially published it in 2011 than a work intended to generate considerable sales. The cliche in job searching is to "market yourself," so it made sense to me to apply marketing principles.

With that said, I've employed a strategy based on Sun Tzu's principles—flexibility while planning.

Here is an example:

> Gillette is world famous for its razors, but the company does not make money on the razors themselves; its profits come from the replacement razor blades. In purchasing the razor, a customer commits him or herself to eventually making repeat purchases of razor blades, which results in a profit for Gillette— hence, the "razor-razor blade" strategy.

May you enter your battles with confidence.

About the Author

Vincent Gagliano is a career banker who has used these ideas to innovate in some most challenging projects in the financial services industry, including underwriting millions of dollars in loans for a subsidiary of Truist, enabling M&T Bank to achieve compliance in a major FDIC regulation, and helping a global bank complete a $100 billion model coverage exercise. He has an MBA from Cornell University and a BS from the University of Florida with Majors in Mathematics and statistics.

Bibliography

America's Game: 1996 Green Bay Packers. Perf. Brett Favre. Warner Home Video, 2006. Hulu.

America's Game: 1998 Denver Broncos. Perf. Mark Schlereth, Terrell Davis, John Elway. Warner Home Video, 2006. Hulu.

America's Game: 2002 Tampa Bay Buccaneers. Dir. Bennett Viseltear. Perf. Jon Gruden. Warner Home Video, 2007. Hulu.

Andretti, Mario, "Mario Andretti Quotes". http://www. quotelucy.com/quotes/mario-andretti-quotes.html Last accessed August 2.4, 201.0

BBC news, "China set to Be Largest economy." BBC news online. http://news.bbc.co.uk/2./hi/business/4998020. stm Last accessed September 28, 2010.

Berra, Yogi, "Yogi Berra Quotes" http://www. brainyquote. com/quotes/authors/y/yogi_ berra.html. Last accessed August 22, 2010.

Berri, Dave. "The Super-star Theory or How to Win an nBA title." http://dberri.wordpress.com/2007/08/05/

the-super-star-theory-or-how-to-win-an-nba-title Last modified August 5, 2007.

Bryant, Paul, "Coach Paul Bear Bryant Quotes".http://www.coachlikeapro.com/coach-paul-bear-bryant.html. Last accessed August 22, 2010.

Bynum, Justin. "What is the Razor-Razorblade Model?" *Investopedia*. http://www.investopedia.com/ask/answers/08/razor-blade-model.asp. Last accessed February 11, 2011.

Davidson, Willie G., *100 Years of Harley-Davidson.* (new York: Melcher Media, Inc., 2002.). 2.32.-2.33, 2.42.-2.43

Douglas, Michael "Greed is Good". http://www.tradingwinner.com/archive/2006/01./2.8/ greed-is-good/. Last accessed August 22, 2010.

Holtz, Lou, "Lou Holtz Quotes". http://thinkexist. com/quotes/lou_holtz/3.html. Last accessed August 22, 2010. http://quotationsbook.com/quote/1.861.7/. Last accessed August 24, 2010.

Kinicki, Angelo and Brian K. Williams. *Management: A Practical Introduction* (4th edition), (new York: McGraw-Hill, 2009) 41.8-19.

Krames, Jeffrey. *Jack Welch and the 4E's of Leadership* (McGraw-Hill Companies, 2005), 2.-3, 6-7, 77, 1.04-05

Lincoln, Abraham, "Abraham Lincoln Quotes." http:// www.finestquotes.com/author_ quotes-author-Abraham%20Lincoln-page-0. html. Last accessed August 24, 2010.

Lombardi, Vince, "Famous Quotes by Vince Lombardi." http://www.vincelombardi.com/quotes.html. Last accessed August 22, 2010.

Maxwell, John. *Everyone Communicates, Few Connect* (nashville: thomas nelson, 201.0), 1.87

Maxwell, John. *The 21 Irrefutable Laws of Leadership, 10th Anniversary Edition.* (nashville: thomas nelson, 2007) 68-69, 1.55-57, 1.87-88.

Porter, Michael. *Competitive Advantage,* (new York: the Free Press: 1985), 1.86-88, 51.4-1.5.

Porter, Michael. *Competitive Strategy,* (new York: the Free Press: 1980), 20-2.1., 45, 84, 94.

"Quotes on Initiative" http://www.leadershipnow. com/initiativequotes.html. Last accessed August 22, 2010.

Silbiger, Steven. *The Ten-Day MBA,* (new York: William Morrow and Company, Inc.: 1993), 32.6-2.7.

Skjevstad, Vegard. "one-Liners." http://vegard.net/ one-liners/. Last accessed August 22, 2010 sonshi.com. *Sun Tzu* "the Art of War". sonshi.com, 1999-201.1.. www.sonshi.com/learn.html. Last accessed August 18, 2010.

"sonshi Forum: Sun Tzu Art of War explained: eleven: nine Grounds" http://forum.sonshi.com/showthread.php?s=&threadid=693.

Accessed August 2.1., 201.0 stokesbury, James L. *A Short History of the Civil War.* (New York: William Morrow and Company, Inc., 1995) 1.59-70.

Tzu, Sun and Gerald A. Michaelson. *The Art of War for Managers: 50 Strategic Rules.* Avon: Adams Media Corp., 2001..

Tzu, Sun. *The Art of War.* translated by Lionel Giles. http://www.chinapage.com/suzi-e.html. Last accessed october 28, 2010.

Notes

9 781958 692349